les poemes philosophique

VOLUME 2

Also by Ivan Kireevskii

Sculptum Est Prosa, Volume 1 – The Voices of Genius
Sculptum Est Prosa, Volume 2 – The Voices of Silence
Sculptum Est Prosa, Volume 3 – The Voices of the Unpeople
Sculptum Est Prosa, Volume 4 – The Voices of the Oceans
and Trees
Sculptum Est Prosa, Volume 5 – The Voices of the Bankers
and the Thieves
The Vase of Suso and the Lost Scrolls of 'J'
Second Decade – Collected Poems (2011-2020)
Les Philosophique, Volume 1 – The Voices of Existentialism

les poemes philosophique

VOLUME II

The Voices of the Heretics and Saints

Ivan Kireevskii

LUMINARE PRESS

WWW.LUMINAREPRESS.COM

Les Poemes Philosophique
The Voices of the Heretics and Saints
Copyright © 2023 by Ivan Kireevskii

Printed in the United States of America

Cover Design by Claire Flint Last

Luminare Press
442 Charnelton St.
Eugene, OR 97401
www.luminarepress.com

LCCN: 2022909727
ISBN: 979-8-88679-322-2

For Michelle, Donna and Sue,

My colleagues and dear friends

Contents

Prologue

In Ivan Kireevskii's second volume of his *Les Philosophique* series, he searches through all the kingdoms of antiquity and of modern times where he draws his creations from out of his own reality… reassembling a body of words, creating a language that may have never existed before.

A language, first aimed at the senses independent of speech in search of feeling for syllable and rhythm penetrating far below the conscious level of thought. His method is to uncover layer after layer, and archaeologise myth from conflated myth.

In discovering metaphors, Kireevskii replaces these categories by concrete links and in so doing intensifies his consciousness of reality. To experience full mystical awareness, he has developed his special use of language by which he maneuvers his consciousness to the borderline where it can draw previously unexpressed parts into the realm of the expressible.

It is said that within poets, the universe becomes subjective; they experience a heightened sense of alienation from their own being. Alienated from his own self, Kireevskii finds the way home and settles into the impossible.

By means of veils and symbols… the products of scraps and aspects of reality, the poet must create a new world not from nothing but from a set of things awaiting composition and arrangement.

The result is a work often more incommensurable and incomprehensible for the understanding. This is Kireevskii's intent as in his words;

"a poem that leaves nothing to be guessed is no true work of art to the beholder."

These poems in Volume 2 are of flesh and blood and often mythical and elusive... philosophical and often very difficult to understand. They fit no literary genre or linguistic structure. They hide layers of meaning quite often in need of deciphering.

To Kireevskii, poems stand like cathedrals in the wilderness; they offer an infrangible dignity, unconsoled clarity, unfenced existence… they are the outward sign of an inner grace; they are examples of self-conquest; they show that the reality of the world should not be underprized; they offer a sense of sufficiency, and a spurt of abundance from a source within.

It has been said that Kireevskii's poems are shapes of a circle of thought. He is sometimes social, sometime political and often philosophical. At times blasphemous, but often spiritual. He will make you angry… he will make you smile. He will make you sad… but mostly, he will make you think.

May you, dear reader, succeed at the hard task of understanding the metaphor and may you catch the varying rhythm and design of each poem.

—Patricia Marshall
Publisher, Luminare Press

Introduction

I must be profoundly related to all the dark abysses in this work where I found the counterparts in my own soul and at times my words amounted to a violation of Euterpe.

It is not doubt, but certitude that drives one mad. But in order to feel this, one must be profound, one must be an abyss, a philosopher… We all fear the truth.

This boundary is the inner unknown… but an inner unknown creating an impression of infinity and all the while doing nothing but delimiting man and forcing him to confront his own boundaries.

Here, with an insatiable and passionate demand, I have made tremendous attempts to solve this problem of modern tragedy to solve the "riddle of the sphinx" and hurl it into the abyss.

It is here that I grab my pen in order do battle with my monsters. Here, the anarchy within instincts of creative and religious forces so energetically desire satiety, such that they cannot be content with the crumbs that fall from the table of modern knowledge.

This protrusion of the impossible should in principle lead to silence. At the same time this is a precondition of poetry.

Each morning without church on the wild cement… I kneel down before nothing. In this rightful place I kneel down before everything and write…

with a silver chalice
of consonants and vowels
burning

scattered fables
beaten by the wind
but chained

a bundle of reflections
left in my hands

i am in the middle
dangling in a cage

i am in the pause
i neither end
nor begin

a syllable
from each broken phrase

the whim
of a speculative god

history…
a coming and going
with no beginning
and no end

shadowless words
i didn't hear them
i denied them

i said they don't exist

footsteps
in my mind
shadows of thought
through the path of echoes

the seen and
the unforeseen

through that frontier of doubt
crossed only
by glimmers and mirages

where language recants
i travel toward myself
i enter the abandoned

threatened
by what i have written

i walk among the images
in a mind
that has lost its memory

i am one of its images
my pencil rebels

i fold the page
whispers…
they are watching me
from the foliage of my words

—Ivan Kireevskii

There are more mysteries contained in the shadow of a person who walks in the sunlight than in all the religions of mankind, past, present, and future.

—Földényi, F. László

I

contours not yet revealed

mysteries
contained in the shadow
unity carved into the stone
o'… that metaphysical order

refute not
the divine
extinguish not
every spark

seek your own face
in the faces
expelled
into nonexistence

sound out the depth
read what is hidden
with the gaze
of a stranger

stare fixedly
into nothingness
into that
alluring metaphor

a kind of net
intricate
unboundedness…
contours not yet revealed

as thoughts
arise
further thoughts…
are lost in riddles

rattling chains
thought long since broken
beware reformers
theoreticians and peddlers

travel the world
wearing a mask
seek out the path
leading only to thyself

... simply rattling chains we thought long since broken, and we could never imagine that in fact Fate had reforged them for us, far stronger and crueller than ever before.

—Zweig, Stefan

II

o' the unfinished temple

confront the sight
of this chasm
within you

facelessness
gazing in
upon itself

do not speak
or disturb…
be silent

questions
of inexpressible
melancholy

piercing fragility
under scrutiny…
hunches abandoned

contempt
for the unexamined
fear of the realm

statues
have lost their paint
their arms… their heads

o' the unfinished temple
at segesta
forsaken on a hill

with wind blowing
between
the unfluted columns

and the sun shining
on grass
flowers and life

the open structure
of plato's thought
or the single-mindedness of thomas

where god
is completely red
and completely green…

i begin to stumble…
deadened acuteness
in veiled aphorisms

whether myths
or inspirations
of the moment

that do not wait
for reason
to inform them

when a man
has a will
ready to believe

he loves
the truth
he believes

even images
in the old cathedrals
can be revered

beware
the conflicts
and common sense

element of acquaintance
stammering's
of the ecstatic

clearing
in the jungle
of existence

the primeval chaos
the hidden
meaning

i throw my creations
into the face
of the world

take them
or leave them
as you see fit

traveling on
this bumpy
and uneven road

... I promise to set forth the views of those who are now teaching heresy... to show how absurd and inconsistent with the truth are their statements... I do this so that... you may urge all those with whom you are connected to avoid such an abyss of madness and of blasphemy...

—Bishop Irenaeus, c. 180

III

grey

that of the silenced
the ones held in secret
the concealed
seeking truth

writings anonymous
falsely ascribed
or forged
yet deemed holy

nobody looks back
from a mirror…
with no explanation
lost behind the finite

passioned… it suddenly
bursts into flame
a conspiracy of silence
bore within itself

colonizing paradise
with weapons
leaving a soul…
empty and maimed

chasms
slashing your existence
into shreds
colored in grey

invented speeches
yellowed by time
cobbled together…
the embryo of the sacred

the tragic wounding
of the human spirit…
here no one dares
battle with the grey

this dark mantle
of night
this… the dethronement
of god

The day when you were given to the world,
At a given order the planets hailed the sun,
And right away you ceased to believe
According to that law which governed your apparition.

… And neither time nor any force can break
The shaped strength which living evolves within.

—Goethe

I V

the image undisguised

spiral terrace
of the wind
follow the path
of your blood

through this empty arch
comes the wind
shattering
the idols of the age

a crown of snakes
intelligence frozen
at their sight…
pages of battling thought

the body struggles
against an invisible midst
and man stands alone
apart from man

the image
undisguised
spoken in sayings
cryptic and compelling

where beliefs
become placeholders
expressed at the other side
of the mind

spontaneous
unconscious thoughts
concealed
unorthodoxy repressed

behind
so many pronouns
lines, silences
zigzags

an ardent struggle
an endless vigil
the dust
of stuffed images

chanted litanies
a cathedral's eye…
here, my words became visible
for a moment

I do not believe my faith to be the one indubitable truth for all time, but I see no other that is plainer, clearer, or answers better to all the demands of my reason and my heart...

—Tolstoy

V

executors of dust

humanized madmen
in cages
of infinity

have swilled it out
of full cups
driving out error with error

stones explode
the air
has turned solid

bandages of dark
cover the eyes
of what you wrote

philosophic acrobatics
and brute inversions
glass… made of air

o' you executors of dust
you…
who stopped me

in the middle
of these
my unwritten lines

piled on my breast…
once the unseen
is now the seen

bliss into pain
and as you are now...
i am too

Most of the ancient forms of [religion] are unknown to people in the world today, since they eventually came to be reformed or stamped out. As a result, the sacred texts… used to support their religious perspectives came to be proscribed, destroyed, or forgotten—in one way or another lost.

—Bart D. Ehrman

VI

galleries of echoes

you and i
once walked in the sunlight
until the light
turned dim
you…
a lamp of emptied oil

let me now
bravely face myself
from this new world
within invented concepts…
a kind of a net

which i was once
forced to conform
to preconceived notions
as something
to be manipulated…
as if a weapon

covering
the bounty of life
awaiting your delectation
a waiting…
yellowed by time
a fate reforged

far stronger and crueler
than ever before
this
your dethronement…

'o faceless one

the virgin page
in one hand
the script immortalized

words
of an aforethought
hampered in there
intensity

tablets once written
by the sun
spoken
with the words of water
never fully understood
never fully felt

i am in a room
abandoned
by language
where logic of passion
recapitulates

figures, motifs, forms, and styles
are seen to interact
in a myriad
of interlinking patterns

i am
dancing on a tightrope
between seriousness and satire
disinherited…
one whom the past
no longer belongs
and not yet the future

you once revealed yourself
to the great as great…
to the small as small
to the aged
as one who has aged

'o faceless one

it is nighttime
two violins are heard
there are many clouds
and my face
has turned the color of ash

the world is deep
deeper than day
where days and gods
have become indistinguishable
unstrained

there are
no stained-glass windows here
only fabrications
written on leaden tablets
and linen cloths

questions are endless
emanated
in a bewildering series
terror
in crushing proportions

i open my eyes
my steps resound
what i say vanishes
between two parentheses

in a scrawl
with ink-stained hands
written and erased
what i once had written

even the sea has lost its speech
i beat
the drum of the moon
my letters
coming and going
through the tunnel
of my eyes

i scratch each line
here
in this hermit's cell
errant numbers
of that spiral
unwinds

i am
the entrance to a tunnel
where space deconstructs itself
and the sun
turns to time…
time turns to stone

i walk
through galleries of echoes
past broken images
facades
and gardens of symbols
humiliated palaces

where finally
night bust into pieces
upon the weight
of this weightless moment

a falsely interpolated pericope
counsel of despair
hanging, as if abandoned…
the void
has widened around me

is this
where society dissolves
where rhythm
is annihilated
where fire, rock, and air
wound each other
and purify themselves

'o faceless one

There is a profound sense of the mystery of personality and tendency to explore it, as it were, from the outside in, always moving from the exterior to deeper and deeper subterranean levels that are only gradually brought to light.

—*Dostoevsky,* by David Frank

VII

grey showers

you do not know
how my world appears
from within…
the unbounded suddenly breaks

my shadow falls
in a square yard of blackness
the undivine
the monotonous, grey hell

no tongues of flame
an unreflected silence
where darkness and its foliage
grow pale

leading me
to the division
against myself…
i meet the exemplars of error

i have seen grey showers
have moved towards the waves
lived within a myth
while believing in no myth at all

through that frontier
of doubt
crossed only by glimmers
and mirages

where
groups of silence
and bones and flutes
resound

a thousand books
to work out
the mysteries
of an indifferent wind

learning its creeds
and revered texts
angel, overman…
orpheus and dionysus

yet, there is a bitterness
a frailty of hope…
i fall
without falling

i hang from a thread
spurning their views
maligning their persons
destroying their words

and as my shadow falls
it dissolves into clarity
alas, as they are
i too am shattered

… reason extinguishes her lamp and we are left in darkness. Only fancy can wander in this darkness and create fiction.

—Emanuael Kant

VIII

rafael

travel beyond virgil
discover truth
within your beast

wander
into a distant night

rise up
set your foreheads
against the ignorant

but not in the guise
of old forms

not in your abyss
of sorrows

the water rises
as the shadow falls
in beatitudes of hunger

on the frayed walls
where you trace
charcoal signs

but the water tastes of dust
o' saint scoundrel saint…
thy conscience of rigidness

there will be no vision
amidst your journey
from darkness and delusion…

blurred boundaries
testaments
and prophecies

you do not absolve
or condemn…
are neither just nor unjust

an explanation of the obscure
by the more obscure
one illusion after another

a stripping away of fantasies
start once
as make-believe

freezing in awe
revelations and abominations
and the vilified nameless

saint clown
saint beggar
rotted idol

'ay, but the soul…
he is rafael'
and i am in the wandering hour

a patriot
of the inner worlds

… philosophical problems remain… after we have disentangled ourselves from the philosophical puzzles…

—Abraham Kaplan

IX

the internecions

words flow from stone
rippling shadows
falsified writings…
heresies

precepts of arrogance
and dogmas, too
evaporating
into utopian reverie

a wavering river
that flows
in doubts and turns
grasping the lie

the virgin
the flame
words of water
fatal error of thought

the inexhaustible texts
a sacred canon
instituted
with blood

the indifferent wind
the virgin
the resurrection
the stone theater

of memory
of presences
formless dizziness
in the cell of god

womb of the temple
savage warfare
the dark walls
of the internecions

The vice of a soul is ignorance; the virtue of a soul is knowledge.

—Hermes

X

plato

sublime myths
and metaphors
mystery rites and
a ghost in chains

revamped and mutilated
hushed in silence
egyptianism and
the rosetta stone

sacrificed
by a dark belief
which no one
understands

writings
excluded and banned
anguished words
hidden in sand

more time
than stone
immobile
abyssed

mixing night
and water
erased… then
started again

in a cone of shadow
spinning flames
backward phrases
puncture time

at the crossroads
of eight directions
its doors
open to the invisible

eternally tossed
between the nearer
and the farther
shore

here, god
and the devil died
to dissolve
the world of being

full immersion
lines at random
and the wind
of the hundred days

vanishing
amid the drought
numbers
in flames

god of
flouting mathematics
and biblical
mosaics

immortal, eternal
and boundless
an unhealed wound
in consciousness

history of tensions
acrimonious debates
scrutinized
as something never said

obscuring
the real
leaving traces
that can never be

writing
not of signs
murmurs where
faithless dust remains

thinkable
imaginable
a god
temple-less

an atom of space
with dire pain
at the source
this… bearing a heart of ice

a garden
of black and red
the dark earth
losing life after life

i hear
the sound of the hours
they are grey and flat
as shadows

beneath the fringes
of the forbidden robe
cross of contradiction
seized the shining grail

framed in disciplines
of fire and ice
twisted, stern
in the radiant limb

altars in decay
profane words
scrawled in black
across the sun

sluggishly surge
where the secret caves
resemble plato…
rugged and dark

somnolent
let there be neither
shadow
nor bower

Man cannot stand a meaningless life.

—Carl Jung

XI

beneath the cold glare

in ruined temples
marble daemons scratch
mute thoughts
on muted walls

wandering steps
of the twenty-seven
carved up fragments
with scissors and paste

beneath the cold glare
a distempered dream
resigned to be
misunderstood

darkness and
rare old words
lacunulose
suppressed and reformed

editors
years removed
re-fitted mosaics
copied and forged

a congeries of doubts
and spurious words
disparately glossed
borrowed from lore

from cloud-capp'd towers
and hallowed graves
all which it inherits
shall be snared and displaced

the irrational themes
reasoning confused
escaping by a
negating self

evasioned sophistries
a wasteland…
preserved in the amber
of allegory

a history
that never occurred
o' the miracles
that were never performed

tragedies
of imprisoned blood
abandoned
by the land of god

even the branches
of ancient trees
are broken and weak
and silent too

… logic is the weak side of history

—Walter Kaufmann

XII

a ceaseless tale

weaving echoes…
of fallen matter
languages stolen
from the abyss

the great collisions
of tragedy
a heavy, chilly breath
of embellishments

sacrifices of
blood and treasure
a momentary flash
and the resurrected god

embodied in egypt's
osiris
and the flawless young
tammuz

a ceaseless tale
of human folly
blindness
and brutality

opening
immortal eyes
inward into
the worlds of thought

a penitentiary pilgrimage
under arms
doomed
to be no more

diverse paths winding
toward the summit…
this fusion of
esoterica

terseness carried
to obscurity
in history's
realm of sin

We now know that at one time or another, in one place or another... noncanonical books and many others were revered as sacred, inspired, scriptural. Some of them we now have; others we know only by name. Only twenty-seven of the early Christian books were finally included in the canon, copied by scribes through the ages, eventually translated into English, and now on bookshelves in virtually every home in America. Other books came to be rejected, scorned, maligned, attacked, burned, all but forgotten—lost.

—Bart D. Ehrman

XIII

my deepest wound

an uncovered cache
altars in decay
profane words
scrawled in black

the unfeeling storm
of a frozen faith
the continuum…
the rhythm of pain

words lost
destroyed and banned
racked between
the fact of doubt

a thin veneer
of an illusory faith
flashed, echoes
untouched and unheard

like water
from a fountain
and the beat
of the sea

history
reinvented
errors have become
thy fictive truth

testaments and prophesies
written and erased…
apparitions
written by the wind

orthodoxy
of one age
heresy
of the next

ah…
you have put
your finger
in my deepest wound

*... genius [is that] crisis that joins the buried self
for certain moments to our trivial daily selves.*

—William Butler Yeats

XIV

two eyes and a twisted rage

of labyrinthine intricacy
so shall they fold the world
the melancholy
long and withdrawing

the roar of the sea of faith
chaos of an ancient night
fleeing from beneath
thy fiery harrow

a cloudy heaven
mingled with stormy seas
in twenty-seven heavens
and all their hells

with chaos
the aztecs knew it
the greeks divined it…
indelible scriptures of the blaze

painted stages
that fell apart by scenes
written by an unknown
a vision rather than doctrine

i walk among the images
ripped up and scrapped
and began again
across the sun

numbers in flames
a wavering river
o' those sketches
of doubt

architectures
built above an abyss
the bewitchment
of intelligence

where a stone
wants to be a shadow…
invisible hands
of symmetry

dark fountains splashing
the faith of dream
taking more delight
in the abstract

the mystic subtlety
a torn cloud
before the hurricane
wind in a scrawl

a foul historical record
promulgated
in falsehood
languages of fallen matter

no picture for the beholder
no symphony for the listener
a fallen beast… with
two eyes and a twisted rage

… various figures, motifs, forms, and styles may be seen to interact within a myriad of interlinking patterns to constitute a vast fabric, which ultimately comprehends much… about human life, about the world, about time, and history, about the ultimate values and the ultimate powers which govern everything in our experience.

—Cyrus Hamlin

XV

of a waveless sea

chaos
and a dancing star
sun has left his blackness
for a fresher day

the contrary
and the unity
seeing the infinite
though weakened and confused

wisdom
hidden in caves and dens
madness and
blasphemy against its own

hollow hand
the unnoticed point of thought
a secret burrow
of the darkest need

of what the thunder said
it contemplates alone
pestilent depths
of a waveless sea

the road's
a thousand lips
dissolving sticks
of a broken cross

disordered sound
and interrupted air
a meaninglessness
of empty creeds

stained pages
and scriptural books
ignorance suppressed
evidence destroyed

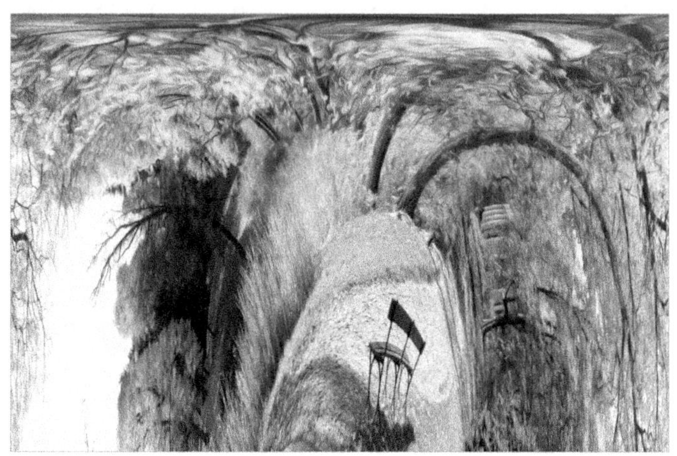

The road to individuation is lonely and rough especially if there is a widespread lack of understanding of even a belligerence toward the mission.

—C.G. Jung

XVI

caves of the weary mind

in caves of the weary mind
doubt replaces certainty
you will hang no withered wreaths
in the sanctuary of life

stand…
o' cathedral in the wilderness
with unconsoled clarity
infrangible dignity

recreate this earth
in terms of your heaven
and as you believe
so do you see

and a spurt of abundance
from a source within
and as you see
so is your earth

ride your horses
and not only horses
but dragons…
constantly interchanging

they lengthen their cord
and go ever backward
shuddering before the sanctuary
of sixteen pillars

weeping every one
at the passages...
the four prophets speak
murmuring, words of air

The natural stage of literalism is that in which the mythical and the literal are indistinguishable... This stage has a full right of its own and should not be disturbed... up to the moment when man's questioning mind breaks the natural acceptance of the mythological versions as literal [and] prefers the repression of their questions to the uncertainty which appears with the breaking of the myth.

—Paul Tillich

XVII

the faith of a dream

can silence
grow inward in
riddled indifference

spilled
on the tablets
where daemons watch

repeated motifs
discarded
in a darkened sky

i wander
i hesitate
upon cheseldon hills

o' river...
drifting in
a swift-passing night

the abstract
and indefinite...
the finite form

expressions
gradations
rugged and dark

ruined temples
jasper tombs
and a mutilated sphynx

an underground river
thunders
in the depths

in search of meaning…
mute thoughts
on mute walls

words in limbo…
the faith
of a dream

The classical philosophical systems... are not to be studied as living organisms, but studied as the curiosities of human thought.

—R.M. White

XVIII

the house of eternity

i shall break myself
into fragments
unconnected…
a haunting is everywhere

unbounded
unfathomable
untrustworthy…
a whirlwind of forms

the windmills
multiply
i sketch the echo
and walk where i've never been

the beasts
crouch in the darkness
clarity effaced
in a syllable

rivers of blood
rivers of history
through the altar
and the knife

sown errors
over the fruitful fields…
still, the house of eternity remains
unknown among the dead

Become what thou art through understanding.

—Nietzsche, *Thus Spake Zarathustra*

XIX

does god yet exist

the search
the secret rhyme
the unknown
from the alone to the alone

knottily complex
strands of entanglements...
fiercely dressed
in transparent dampness

ambiguity on trial
a theater of
the dramatized...
tablets and manuscripts

axis
of the solstices
vague
and unresolved...

to be
both priest and victim
to scratch a line
in the hermit's cell

a line that never
stops writing itself
pausing on the edge
of vaulted domes

where there is nothing
that cannot be erased
you draw your portrait
then find nothing

time splits open
foam of fear
covers your cheeks
here's where you ask…

*... besides the real or actual physical world of our ideas,
there exists a third world, inhabited by thoughts to which
the attribute 'objective but not actual' could be applied.*

—Brian McGuinness

X X

aeterna veritas

illusions
of truth
priests who
beat with the cross

lost knowledge
standing
at the summit
and abyss

melancholy splendors
complex and rich
polemical tractates…
a jury of phantoms

inseparable from
the knower and the known
inquiry snared
caught, and taken

the prophet's
metaphor
a thread
of clarities

long chains
of the abstract
illusions unshaken…
aeterna veritas

If God had looked into our minds, he would not have been able to see there whom we were speaking of.

—Ludwig Wittgenstein

XXI

hymns of blood

at an infinite distance
in the corner's day
sunk to
empurpled rage

the effect
is numbing
dogma turned fierce
violence… like fire

a quenchlessness
a hunt for essence
in holy words…
o' blasphemy

ancient and arcane
where west winds sigh
and they ruin even
the divinest things

archetypal images
and symbols
dramatic books
prophets and essenes

of this
medieval night
beneath the stories
are allegories and myth

the others
so faceless
reading what they
ought not to have read

the philosopher
stares back
unfettered
unscathed

the lingering shadows
of homelessness
storm and darkness
reconciled

eyes talked
into blindness
submerging words
at the edge of itself

a mortal mystery…
the ninth sphere
hymns of blood
and mockery

false disputants
two dark serpents
indivisible…
in tangled dust

*Philosophy is not the search for truth and knowledge or as
a struggle against ignorance and error. It is a battle against
the bewitchment of our intelligence...*

—Renford Bambrough

XXII

mute as a shadow

my memory weaves
running
against the walls
of my cage

tinged with
the red dawn
deepened
in its pathos

the contradictions
of chilled realities
the bludgeon
of self-deception

shallow interpretations
disguised
in a poisonous
kantian robe

statues
carved from wood
pouring water
over gilded images

a raging torrent
chaotic and confused
changing patterns
in literary form

a shuddering voice
of hoarse despair
rapt imagination
inverted and cold

with blasphemy
for prayer
poisonous rust
into the soul

in the caves
at ajanta
eternity mocks…
its pathless wilderness

reason sacrificed
the storm of vibrations
stumble…
mute as a shadow

... as the history of literature testifies throughout, everything of value takes a long time to gain authority, especially if it is of the instructive and not of the entertaining sort; and meanwhile the false flourishes.

—Arthur Schopenhauer

XXIII

between grey and grey

of a person
who walks in the sunlight
engaged in
insight of truths

a walker of air
the receiver of texts
moving half a sentence here
the other half there

the difference
between
the instant and
desert hills

you come and go
between
the stolen
and your own

the opening
of the first eye
homeless and
restless

scurrying clouds
stormily
from the denseness…
a distempered dream

rhythmical breathing
inertially human
of gnarled roots
of ancient pines

unavailing gloom
and ponderous chains
a pathless wilderness
remains

the great terrace
of the shwe dagon
the cold world
and their colder minds

the comfort of
a remedial myth…
who really wrote
matthew, mark, luke and john

there are vicious moments
one could not
mitigate or excuse…
left largely ignored

'til understanding dawns
anathematizes errors
for which the heretics
will crouch and pay

a saving sorceress
in the frame of fiction
comes to life
to overcome death

where faith
is not denied
or blessed
but merely exposed

the grey sky
of abstraction cracks
as if by lightning…
a refusing to obey

the secret mysteries
and waterless canals
the nine muses…
one separation away

i watched sophia
stretch forth her hand
followed it into
the region of chaos

truth came not naked
but in types and images
formed from terror
companioned with pain

as parables
to the blind
in fury and passion
i made my voice heard

a suppressed current
a river driven underground
at the edges
of the fallen

i sank like a stone
into the abyss of destiny
the mists redescend
upon the story of life

the shadow of a night
illumined only
by orphic flashes
in which intelligence is drowned

invisible theatre
labyrinthine underways
massing the clouds
entangling the threads

the secret caves
where the dark tale
of hope unfolds
reunioned in a raging tide

a solitary scribe
submerged beneath
his dying words
now stands alone

in conflict
beneath
enticing skies
of destiny

of self-inflicted tortures
of lost faiths
of decomposition…
marooned on a desolate shore

each earthquake
destroyed
the edifice of convictions
more tensed… more defiant

an awe-inspiring silence
no hermit…
blasphemy for prayer
and canonized blood

a raging cataract
it terrifies
it does not dazzle
but it slays

scorched
by my own ardors
sunstruck
by my own rays

carbonized
in my own flames
the falcon swoop
of thoughts clashing

dropping out of step
with the rhythmic pulse
i looked
behind and beyond

mystical visions
dark passages
cryptic narratives
unconnected folktales

where i sought…
beneath the surface
to the ghost
between grey and grey

… it is Maya, the veil of deception, which covers the eyes of mortals, and causes them to see the world of which causes the them to see a world of which one cannot say either that it is or that it is not…

—Ancient Wisdom of the Indians

XXIV

empty seats

of every word
every invented world
enriched in eloquence
heightened in shallowed myth

in the rapture of fire
expressed in our longing
for what
you can never prove

casting a dialogue
impulses of the imagined
a series of strophes
words between various shades of light

arising from the enslaved
in a single line
unlike
what was handed down

where the struggle
and the consciousness
of one's omnipotence
is undecided

while this notion
alternates
between the private
and the cosmic

and south winds
grip us
in a blazing forest
a melody of outlasted form

and thunders
of prophecy
read the face
of the sky

beliefs shattered
in the tumult
to a finish
before empty seats

—Angelus Silesius

XXV

a robe of rubies

i will preach
to the trees and rocks
voyaging
through the seas of thought

i shall deny
alter and creed
and demons who have fled
to the present age

broken where
the winds don't fall
between virtue and fault…
where even the leaves don't breathe

the nuptial age
of days dissolved
and night that teaches
its truth by halves

delusion
and a snare
of vulgar fables
and a hundred creeds

to obscure
and conceal
from flight's roguery
in the shadow's blood

forever voyaging
through the seas of thought
to the tortured cries
of the myth of er

chaos
replaced by rhetoric
this inner darkness
of enlightenment

the meshes twisted
blind and shackled
incoherence and
divided fragments

one-thousand poisons
of bread and wine
hidden under
a robe of rubies

Your foot itself erased the path behind you,
and above it stands written: impossibility.

—Friedrich Nietzsche

XXVI

the sorrow of souls

bring your ear
close
to my brow
and listen

i have seen
in the nether regions
of the imagined…
plains of burning sand

destined
to a flood of heresies
stretched
from the sorrow of souls

where nerves
change into marrow
senses turn inward
to an obliteration of knowledge

without shadow
a crossing
of the universe
through to its darkest depths

descending from
the mount mystery
a terror induced
disguised vision

the destiny
from which we
have already begun
to dissolve

a catechism
for weak minds
invoking demons
who should have fled

i write
an inimical tone
in an all too insolent
and defiant manner

to proceed with
what is demanded
to run frantically
and breathlessly

to wait
for the moment
of its birth
and redemption

creativity in
tutelary mythmaking
liberating itself…
o' you bishops and priests

ignorance, confusion
roadlessness
in the eruptive chaos
of fierce metaphors

embodied in
the insight of the seer
the esoteric meaning
buried deeply within

on a papyrus
of formulas
acted out and retold
in which life is concealed

arguments
alternating with myths
to the god
beyond god

and forests leaping
from image
to image
from thought to thought

until the inner man
has been consumed
and the drama is played
of this spiritual storm

like my shadow
from which alone
the thunderstorm
could burst

holding
friendly converse
with marble statues
of the gods

the hunter circulated
in the blood of the hunted
the pitches down
upon the water to wine

a twelfth hour
in which enlightenment
and destruction
occur simultaneously

filled with despair
torturous self-hatred
instead of the
external unknown

this mad error
from which both
the body and the soul
lie sickened

*The question of whether something like being can be attributed
to gods at all, without destroying everything divine.*

—Michael Millerman

XXVII

between virtue and fault

did i tell you
about the storm…
the rain poured down
in slanting streaks

the narration
arbitrarily
cut loose
from a tangled moment

the tension
of my cloud
and the lightnings
i have cast

hidden beyond
the altar's dust
confronted by
what's unknown

to the lone shores…
i am a guest
following
where i must flee

obscure tracks
and clues
the bounding line…
the infinite

wisdom pregnant
disentangling
a medieval poem
the hidden flower of the sea

unconsciousness
swallowing the dragon…
this conjecture…
drinking its bitterness

beams creak
from desperation
of nails and screws
trying to emerge

rushed shrinking
beneath the dark net
revisionary warfare
the mosaic allusion

the baseness piety
unable to tolerate
between heresy
and orthodoxy

the contour of the canon
sometimes harsh
suppressed, forgotten
or destroyed

doctrines
redefined
the middle ground
between virtue and fault

dire confusion
till the battle fades
a daemon
or the higher self

they don't understand
imagination
they don't understand
the forms and the verse

a narrative
created out of sync
with no roof
no protected realm

a mode of thought
an unbridled dream
weaving into its
darkened imagery

[The goddess] Diana practices her hunting, that is, she participates in Mind, and spends her time exclusively in hunting and understanding.

—Giles of Viterbo

XXVIII

the edges of stones

the most hostile
elements
lying quietly side by side

what cannot be said
yet is manifest…
gives rise to error

forever voyaging
through the seas
of thought

beyond the limits
found
along the edges of stones

time
with one dimension
torturing itself

the miserable sum
from the inner
depth of will

multiplying
and dividing
the infinite by the infinite

thy geometric truth
of the excessive
width of spheres

of its reality…
pervasively vague
and indefinite

We are moved to discover the infinite effect of the infinite cause, the true and living footprint of the infinite vigor, and we have a teaching that tells us not to seek divinity outside ourselves, but within, more deeply inside us than we are ourselves.

—Giordano Bruno

XXIX

shattered spells

the hallowing of truth
wide and deep
visions
and exalted myths

a breath
made of nothing
an empty chapel
silence and shattered spells

the marble
the index of mind
scattered things converge
like a thing unknown

folds of consequences
a sky behind
green and dark
i struggle through the undone

peak and abyss
now merged as one
o' bring me the answer
to dissolve my doubt

hobbling on
through the darkness
my foot itself
has erased its path behind

statues
on cathedral steps
standing speechless…
the orchestra has stopped

Let them search and search again, tirelessly extending
the frontiers of their happiness, those alchemists of the
gardener's art! Let them offer sixty, a hundred thousand
florins reward to whoever realises their ambitious projects!
I though, have found my black tulip, my blue dahlia!

—Baudelaire

X X X

of a waveless sea

chaos
and a dancing star
sun has left his blackness
for a fresher day

the contrary
and the unity
seeing the infinite
though weakened and confused

wisdom
hidden in caves and dens
madness and
blasphemy against its own

hollow hand
the unnoticed point of thought
a secret burrow
of the darkest need

of what the thunder said
it contemplates alone
pestilent depths
of a waveless sea

the road's
a thousand lips
dissolving sticks
of a broken cross

disordered sound
and interrupted air
a meaninglessness
of empty creeds

stained pages
and scriptural books
ignorance suppressed
evidence destroyed

*A sacrilegious and false concept of the physical universe
has dimmed, like a cataract, the intellectual sight of man.
It is necessary first to remove with a strong and charitable
hand this opaque secretion which conceals from him the
real world of vision.*

—O.V. de L. Milosz

XXXI

lingering on

my soul
is overfull
the stars are too far
myths materialize
they vanish, struggle
and fail

passions descend
upon hungry minds
wisdom sleeps
without dreams
and disappear

in the proud billowing
the mime's become
a statue
of shadowy stone

encountering
my identity
for the first time
i neither speak
nor weep

the world dissolves
in an unquiet trance
the sacred
is not always
on the side of truth

the theme
of presence
in its inverted form…
its isolation
its subtraction

the infallible
is circling
towards the sky
and nowhere at all
this misleading echo
of the dream

and shadows
of earth
a space enlarged
by the emptiness
like an abundant hour
starting and striking
to an end

narrative
and revelation
is still detained
in mystery…
fallacious recourse
to the sacred

upon my children's brow
dark falsehood
to disarm
their mind
a boundless chaos
wild and vast

left feeling
forsaken
the transcendence
of the self
interrogates

tragedies
rifts
irresolvable paradox…
neither man, nor angel
nor god

prophecies indicted
by measured dimensions
in the halls
corridors, chambers
passages and stairways
in the great gizeh

foibles, follies
cruelties, fallacies
impostures and falsities
deluded and reckless
the rude and ignorant
barbarians

the murks
of darkness
empty formularies
uncomprehended rituals
a truce without peace
lingering on
in silence

*It's the doubt that takes one at first abominate the intruder,
which wares different from the ecstasy and the feasts the
priest knows, who vainly puts on the vacuity of insignia,
in order to, nevertheless officiate.*

—Stéphane Mallarmé

XXXII

it is written

like a waterfall
of a thousand roaring torrents
of wild confusion
so varied
are the exploits

the devastating hand
of fanatical pietism
closed upon
and crushed within

never been known
buried in
the wrack and debris

half in discernment
and half in blindness

obscure words…
fiction
written by forgers

who
have invented the tales
where nothingness itself
has gained form

acoustical
and meaningless
verses and texts
a rupture between

experience and expression
the profound
the concrete
and the abstract

it does not create
it does not destroy
re-forges the links
between what does and
does not exist

have you become
entangled
in the unfathomable
of the spectator

become
the mysterious heart
black with rage
of this flashing fire

There were rocks and spectral forests. Bridges across emptiness and that broad gray blind pond suspended above its distant bottom like a rainy sky above a landscape. And between gentle, forbearing meadows, appeared the pale strip of the single path, laid out like a long bleaching place.

—Rainer Maria Rilke

XXXIII

the concealing

man
driven, desperate, dismembered
a specter of divinity
and a seventh day of rest

statues of isis and horus
roman lupercalia
by ceremony and miracle
by myth and fear and hope

silent secrets
not to be glimpsed
by the uninvited
in this dark journey

there is
an epic grandeur
sullied
with superstition and cruelty

clay excrement
folly and chaos
a sculptured creator
of hammered hardness

i have travelled
this path
it is a circle
the mysterious… indistinguishable

was i put forth
on these rocks
among the clouds
to tremble

disfigured
by the fallacies
of logic
a counter-rhythmic rupture

nature exaggerates
it distorts… it leaves gaps
the conceptual web
is spinning

the concealing
shadows of dusk
thunder…
and heavenly fireworks

still, voices of beauty
speak gently
on a thousand
bridges and paths

o' life
into the unfathomable
a pressed flower
between the pages i have read

For that which lures us to his feet
Has circled him now a million years,
He has forgotten all we must endure,
encloses all we would escape.

—Rainer Maria Rilke

XXXIV

giordano

a devil
awaits you
while this other god
confronts you too

your words
they burn
not written…
awaited, still

of more than man
a beggars voice
desert hills
and a fallen tower

struggling
impotence
spread forth
in silent-ness

o' sawtooth
hunchback
you split the sky
in shadowing smoke

they stood before…
this hooded friar
bringing down
the core of earth

cartload
of pitch
ten cardinals
and an iron chair

the storm was set
the judge was robed
a secret chamber
and dissembled fraud

in their holy dread
they weighed nothing
in weakening voices
of an invisible choir

mingled
with darkness
dragged
in blood and mud

to the void
woven from within
supernatural shades…
unholy dread

charges, bloody…
false and cold
as curses shook
from a wretched throne

amidst
the waves
and fountains
and the hush of night…

your soothing words
were weaved with skill
in a beggar's voice…
i understood

These words I saw inscribed in some dark color Over a portal. "Master," I said, "make clear their meaning, which I find too hard to gather." Then he, as one who understands: "All fear Must be left here, and cowardice die.

—Dante Alighieri

XXXV

in a creed outworn

monsters and riddles
a heavenly child
a hidden serpent
and irrational ways

a hundredfold mirror
i caught a glance
and its eyes
they spoke

revolting conclusions
on the everlasting theme
grinding teeth
so silent and weak

disfigured
by fallacies
blinding floods
through root-shaped cracks

the unknown
the ungraspable
stones polished
under crashing waves

it coexists
with the nothing
o' barren
and unfettered sea

the empty chapel
jealous god
in the vomit of fury
o' what the thunder said

i will show
in a handful of dust
a desert suckled
in a creed outworn

standing there
dark and naked
the triumphal hymn
of this final dance

a spinning image
distantly unfolds
spiritual acrobat
vertigo of soul

surpassing notes
scribbled in haste
a sacred fire
in an age of ice

The text may indeed be ferociously difficult, but the effort will be repaid by the excellence of the ideas it contains. Keep reading! If you are tenacious and intelligent, you shall be rewarded.

—Ivan Soll, Introduction to *Discovering the Mind*

XXXVI

theft of fire

i summon
the lady of the rocks
to assist
my staggering mind

there is much undoing
to get done
i have even read
her created texts

they are written
like words
still ripening
in silence

like shadows
infallibly circling
where centuries
pass it by

i am unable
to grasp
or to tear
the latter's veil

is death to her
merely a fiction
a narratable event
or unutterable curse

born on the storm
neither matter
nor substance
the last redoubts of the wind

the abyss
of my being…
i spin
on the circle

cruel holiness
invented realm
and the redemptive
drops of blood

i crawl poorly
and weakly along
i shudder
eyes dilated… muscles cramped

in the maze
of my unconscious
this gulf, this void
of the senseless

o' princess of peace
affirmer
dripping with sweat
you have spread your spirit

like the sail
of a castaway
of corrupted worlds
ablaze in empty despair

who soon will turn
to nameless dust
the bottomlessness
of the empty heavens

the theft of fire
phantoms
and illusions…
the last smoke

Few people know their own minds.
Many, though by no means all, would like to.

—Walter Kaufmann

XXXVII

a paper life

an unbridgeable
precipice
between things
and words

a language
of two-dimensions
and most of it
never seen

a paper life
where in every journey
we return
to a single point…

a lightning
of the unknown
indifferent
to the wind

a silence
that is neither
out of the shadow
nor for the shadow

the impossible
scattered
in thought…
nothing written

a parabolic mirror
that cracks the sky
refuting
your inner world

full of phantoms
full of illusions
it exaggerates, it distorts
it leaves gaps

the last breath
of evaporating reality
almost as if
it had never been

where… if you have
nothing to create
then perhaps
you must create yourself

You are deceived by statesmen, priests and the teachers of morals... how you like to adore it. Even today there's, alas, little worth thinking and saying that does not grievously flout mores, the state, and the gods.

—Goethe

XXXVIII

it is written (2)

a shadow
elevated

not at all
copernicus
or einstein

nor even
the vision
of ezekiel

stepping before
doorways
where even the doorposts
tremble

the tranced spirits
strike
they trod forth

a creator
who has made
a time space cage

but, alas
unknown and old

the sinister element
inheres
in secrecy

credulous rabble
as new writings

debased
and disfigured
crude and colorless

i shall read them
not

Between a Tungusic shaman and a European prelate... between the entirely sensuous Mongol who in the morning places the paw of a bear skin on his head with the brief prayer, "Don't slay me!" to the sublimated puritan and independent in Connecticut there is, to be sure, a powerful difference in manners but not in the principle of believing...

—Immanuel Kant

XXXIX

we are all heretics now

the churches
to which
i do not belong

to the void
from which
they are woven

lofty mansion
of ennobling
miscarriage couched on the threshold

foisted upon
stygian darkness
teeth of savage stone

menacing
haunting dogmas
which eat our hearts

out of such quiet
i crept
from their disenchanted woods

destruction
at the heart of chaos
uprooted and broken

life bursts its bound…
breathless, pale
and unaware

i wander
through greyness…
my time is growing dim

the voice of the sphinx
no longer hiding
its eternal riddle

of whirlwind…
whose fierce blasts
the waves and clouds confound

an accumulation
crude allegories
in the realm of forms

o' let the peace of madness flee
until the shades
of evening weep

oppressor's wrath…
angel
of the blind and dead

the deep seat
of my existence
of wrinkled and motionless time

where the lost flower
is devoured
by an empty god

wistful
obstinate
we are all heretics now

Ignorance is ignorance; no right to believe anything is derived from it. No reasonable person will behave so frivolously in other matters or rest content with such wretched grounds for his opinions... Where questions of religion are concerned people are guilty of every possible kind of intellectual misdemeanor and lack of candor.

—Sigmund Freud

X L

calm talk beneath the sphere

stories written
with invisible words
a voice of crystal and steel

thirst
in the syllables
that touch fire in the sound of dark

for whom did you sing

i have taken
one-hundred words from you
i can neither think nor write

two bleeding contraries
dismantling
a once solid form

sealing my lips…

my pen
falls to the floor
chains like mist melt away

the primitive
the naked, the ignorant
the deprived and depraved

words devoid of meaning

feel the silence sink
over the dust
of prophets and kings

caring not
what others think… or
what they do not believe

with half a step i stands still

the nature
of the universe
has no answer

existence
lacks a center
it exaggerates, it distorts… it leaves gaps

in shades of vanished days

mysteries
of when we came
where we lived and whether we ever return

yet we morn
the absurdities
for which men have died

prolonging calm talk beneath the sphere

*… ancient gnostic theologians attempted nothing less
than to chart the whole mind of god.*

—Bentley Layton, *The Gnostic Scriptures*

XLI

tragic in its graces

the gnostic heresy
preceding elohim
a spirit
that animates eternity

inventing the tale…
of fiction
forged
in measureless prose

absurdity
raising an echo
faint and hollow
drama, symbol and rite

kingly slaves
arrayed in gold
blood…
and questioning looks

i have seen the sun at midnight
shining brightly
i have entered
the presence of the gods below

seen the dull sadness
of monasteries…
the emptiness
in their souls

inflicted madness
on the borderline
between the being
and the non

darkness
leaping out
and around...
tragic in its graces

Horus the saviour, who was brought to birth as light in heaven and sustenance on earth... who paved the way of resurrection to eternal day. Lord of two worlds, united and made one.

—*The Egyptian Book of the Dead*

XLII

i leave eternity to thee

swift shadows
over my eyes
have shed
the idle winds

restless clouds
before the steadfast sun
under this broken stone
i halt

the past has come
in aberrance
even obscure
where the lifeless silence sleeps

thy oracle's
detained…
o' that soothsayer stood
outside time

surrounded by a world
of untruth
its shallows and depths
unholy and profane

the path
of initiates
into inner mysteries…
undecipherable

to riddles…
beyond gods
where there is nothing empty
and nothing too full

unsolvable secrets
conjectures and dreams
a lonely temple
in an unhallowed land

o' holy event
undo your shrine
fabricated and foisted
upon the gullible

archaic philosophy
has sealed the lips
muting as well
the pulpit voice

shadowed
for centuries
the dark malignancy
of triumphant error

sun-gods and avatars
of the ancient world
dismantling
the once solid fabric

cut so deeply
at the very roots
of the tree of faith
that its leaves and branches

withered and enveloped
in stygian darkness…
that lofty mansion
of ennobling conception

foisted upon
a credulous rabble
the slurs
and slights

the voice
of the sphinx
no longer hiding
its eternal riddle

hollow mockery
beguiling hallucination
of shallow
and banal exotericism

a cold abstraction
the glyphs, symbols
lying in
the mystery chests

lamps casting
a broad shadow
of the sleeping warrior
blankness of no meaning

i leave
eternity to thee
not the dignity of kings
nor robed investiture

but that abounding dignity
which has
the most mournful
perchance... the most abased

among them all
in a colorless landscape
formed in fright...
i leap into darkness

*I recognized I was a substance whose whole essence or
nature is to think and whose being requires no place and
depends on no material thing.*

—Descartes

XLIII

into the dark

i shout a secret
to the stone
and let its cry
distracts my thoughts

an inquiring soul
exploring the dark
hoarding its wisdom
and a part of its truth

saturn cannot
easily signify
the divine or brutish
the blessed or bowed down

i set a trap
for existence
but they who fell into it
became worldless

there the world
broke up
into worlds
with separate entrances

where god was hiding
incandescence cooled
my genius foisted
irresolvable contradictions

i constantly
at every moment
endangered myself
and kept falling

spiraling down
to ever-greater depths
here excess
could not be constrained

here the world
found its own center
everything condensed
into one

i have chosen
the serpent
as my guide
i have traded wisdom

just to dance
in the street
where boundaries
shoot out into the dark

It is of prime importance to distinguish the fact that the use of a "true" always glances backwards or forwards to the actual or envisioned making of a statement by someone, from the theory that it is used to characterize such (actual or possible) episodes...

—P.F. Strawson

XLIV

the ghost of my heart

scatter rationalism
to the winds
grind your teeth
in silent impotence

think about
the being of beings
the manifestation
of the hidden

the ancients
called it chaos
a form of absence
that completes existence

join then
your hands and hearts
let the shapes
of this scenery shift

as time
is part of the world
and reason
the search of a truth

existing now
or coming into existence
that it is the part
which generates time

truth
which is not revealed
could not exist
without your glance

treading
proserpine's threshold
i passed through the elements
and returned

the force
of the feeling
of emptiness and infinity
creatureliness and noncreatureliness

the sinister element
inhered in this secrecy
menaced by
her haunting dogmas

this mystery cult
apologies in the morning…
i stand barefoot
in the snow all night

the ghost of my heart
changes and dissolves
like pores
blown into hot rock

my sword
and my shield
glitter in its light…
yet this is nothing

all
that i have said and done
o' this rocky voice
circle shaped and still

this part of truth
from an iris bow
the message mute
and undisclosed

bleeding contraries
equally true
pitted against my
inward reason

forbidding man
from what i have taken
i have planted
a false oath

blind and aged
bent, wept
and the heavens…
and then my hours are numbered

my solitude
makes them fragile
this invisible vault
of the void

divine geniuses
that we can neither see
nor hear
the secret things about which i write

astonished
at my own words
and do not even
recognize them

supporting
and piercing the globe
through which the axis
emerges and vanishes

unfounded being…
the song of the sirens
the harmony
of the spheres

the howling
of the wind
the breaking
of the waves

the crashing of stones
in laughter, in sighing
the echo…
the blood streaming

being finally exposed
to the prophecy of being
discovering oneself
in the unknown

in tense and touching moments
which appear utterly grave
despite the gaping absence
in their wake of chaos

in crushing moments
rare and isolated
a gaze
like lightning

the affirmation of the negated
the comprehension
of the incomprehensible
the utterance of the unutterable

to sink
into luxurious inertia
accursed in the laws
of consciousness

only to look about…
blood is being spilt
in streams… unforgotten…
my dreams move drearily

'pour me now into thy bold billows
of my whole foregone life'
where i long to go higher
from all my furthest bounds

where truth is inwrought
is myth, allegory, drama
parable, fable…
a violent welter of forces

an abstract conception
striking my soul
dramatized…
an inner eye of thought

where the secret sanctities
of its wisdom
are invaded
by barbarian crudity

and its treasures of sacred
are wantonly torn out
and exposed recklessly
to the degrading embrace

the dead ghost of truth
in the shape of dark riddles
o' that my imagination…
may fill this gap

To ask if a category is true or not must sound strange to the ordinary mind; for a category apparently becomes true only when it is applied to a given object, and apart from this application would seem meaningless to inquire into its truth. But this is the very question on which everything turns.

—Georg Wilhelm Friedrich Hegel

XLV

beneath veils of allegory

of its cunning spring
of imagination
poverty
and conceptual light

here...
the myths stand
in majesty
and liberated thought

ultimate depths
to the unshadowed soul
excluded from
temple and church

the world
broken up...
in separate doors
fragile and torn

where we step
barefoot
on dampened ground...
we sink in

breaking ourselves
into pieces
before we know
what we are

a flirtation with nothing
silence bursting
filling the air
o'er thy troubled mind

the story stands
in naked form
a somber heave
at parting roads

a misunderstood
outward nature
pitted against
inward reason

destiny broken
bursting through
the boundary
of this fluctuating earth

caught in a relentless wheel
with fifty mirrors
a leaf loosed
from the scroll of time

a hundred eyes
behind god's mask
here i have found
naked truth…

where existence is
but a series
of transient interpretations
of chaos

and being is becoming…
becoming is innocent
a concealment
beneath veils of allegory

When the paths traced out become too difficult, or when we see no path, we can no longer live in so urgent and difficult a world. All the ways are barred. However, we must act. So we try to change the world, that is, to live as if the connection between things and their potentialities were not ruled by deterministic processes, but by magic.

—Jean—Paul Sartre

XLVI

if god is in hiding

i beheld
three red swords
flashing
in the unrisen sun

i beheld
the thunder, the abyss
the trident, the torch
the serpents and the thyrsi of the gods

coming
out of the dark
as i kept watch
with impotent rage

i walked barefoot
into profane space
i walked among men
as among fragments of time

i saw
the soul
released from the senses
turning in upon itself

i heard
the holy ghost
uttering dark speech
in parable form

i took
the veils and wraps
and colors and gestures
away from men

i chose
the serpent for a counselor
wisdom
for a dance in the street

i read white
but they read black
here, the secrets
of my soul were written

i smuggled sense
into the world...
what a price
to break out of existence

i have unplanted
the false oath
to forge the curbs
of iron and brass

i became
the unknown and alien
trespassing into the world
to place it beside itself

i prostituted
its glory
and every gleaming revelation
into tawdry commonplace

i attacked
into the unknown
with the insane fury
of ecclesiastical zeal

i wept
bent
blind and aged
i became worldless

to reach
the most revolting
conclusions…
the everlasting theme

as if god
is in hiding…
is neither faraway
nor divine

i crushed
the foul and false
trampled loose rock
until his grasp was broken

in dream, scepters
and crowns
found beneath his feet
amongst ghastliest forms

repressed faith
an obscene worm
distorted into caricature
a visage changed into darkness

i contemplate
beyond the universe
from afar
the position of eternal exclusion

i have not fallen victim
to the charms
my heart beats
even in silence itself

i found
books filled
with anxieties, deceptions
grief and evil

and then
the horsemen came
and all was done
swifter than my words were spoken

I came to find my mind's disorder sacred.

—Arthur Rimbaud

XLVII

o' hate... thou art

o' you rare
and strange one
your airy gaze...
darkness scales your holy wall

towards the four faces
of humanity...
where
shall i hide

whoever
hears my song
a torrent
of unanswerable questions

i sit apart
in the middle of the universe
fragile and fallible...
the form of the formless

that point in space...
an argument place
that infinite boundary
discoverable everywhere

the solid ground
vanishes
surrendering to the attraction
of nothingness

the sound, tense
and silent
conjured up
by hamlet's final words

the saddest truth
more job
than macbeth…
impulse of wounded dignity

once guided
by a solid world
must i give up
on being myself

a measure
of the measureless
one number
of the unnumbered

from the sanctum
of arcane holiness
under a mass
of the irrational

truth contorted
into untruth
and unknown
even to ourselves

allegories
with the penetrating rays
letters
of the mystical

viewing
the rational
a sudden revelation
that crushed me

a distant light
in a dark forest
hidden
in the depths of my heart

torn
up by the roots
and lay about me
scattered, broken, trampled

crudity of meaning
thwarting
even true intent…
shying at shadows

pursuing
and clinging to phantoms
the turbid mélange
growling at reflections

loud cries
of scorn
idolatry
enriched by myths

stifled torrents
into the dark
in the midst i paused
o' hate… thou art

For every truth that accepts its dependence in regard to narrative and revelation is still detained in mystery; philosophy exists solely through its desire to tear the latter's veil.

—Alain Badiou

XLVIII

eternal riddle

plunged
into the eternal riddle
i rode god
into farness

o' this wanderer…
of barriers and boundaries
where existence
is broken

a tempestuous sea
the obsession of thought
a divinity
in a blue and distant place

our last ride
over human hurdles
they ducked
they wrote… they lied

the unholy
banishment
which gathered up
the scattered ones

o' thy conflict
of pains and upheavals…
come with knife and cup
to drain his blood

nail him down
upon a rock
catch his shrieks
in cups of gold

bind iron thorns
around his head
pierce both
his hands and feet

let the battle
become ghastlier
where few come within
the compass of my curse

bestride the earth
in monstrous
and frightening masks…
where images of fantasy float

come
numbering
your ave-maria's
with your beads of tens and threes

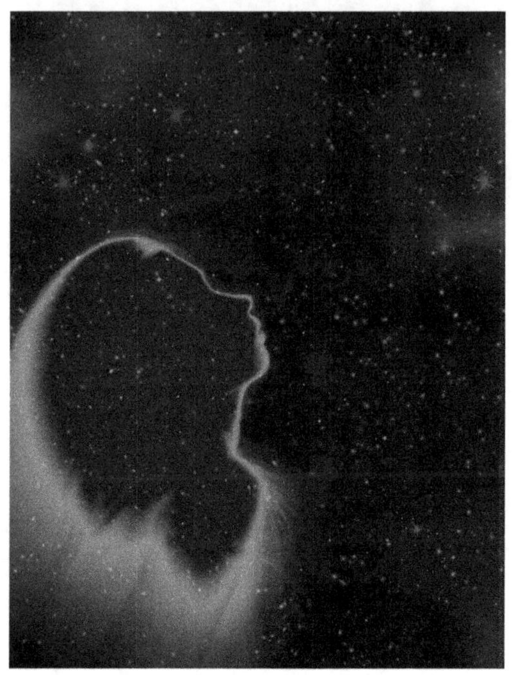

*The 'heavens' and the 'hells' are appearances created by the
inner condition of the spirits themselves, flexible according
to every change or thought, every passion and desire.*

—Emanuel Swedenborg

XLIX

shapes of death

every land
and dogma
is left standing
dispirited and discouraged

the gems
of the soul…
eternal image
and a martyr's groan

the tearing out
of the living heart
thy goddess grows young
as she grows old

captivated
by a mirror
an initial
and a terminal state

the eternal form
shall never renew
here uncertainty
prevails

the encounter
no less abysmal
than estrangement
contradictory in essence

peregrinations
and battles
of an insatiable spirit
and its sense of shame

existence
in imagination
darkness thickened
as the light's withdrawn

hollow out
dimmed away
untamed appetite
of the beast

silhouette vividly
against its light
shapes of death
in the shadow of eve

... the orthodox have been forced to regard their makers as madmen or heretics: when they were really only practical men struggling to disclose great matters by imperfect means.

—Evelyn Underhill

L

a thousand names

black glass
over exhausted eyes
a voluntary blindness
on a darkened ocean shore

unfamiliar vibrations
the weight of the weightless
gnashing
in fierce despair

words
as they echo
dupery of
ecclesiastics

the monster
of mediocrity
parading through
divine space

searching for
a short-cut to wholeness
confronting the
cognoscenti

arcane
books of wisdom
the hallucination of
the millions

slow the cadence
until the words
expose, contradict
deny and vilify

decorative illusions
and a thousand names…
where your gods are remade
in reverence and fear

The more clear the light, the more does it blind the eyes of the owl, and the more we try to look at the sun the feebler grows our sight and the more our weak eyes are darkened.

—St. Catherine

L I

the forest's shiver

secrets
with a lying gloss
before the darkened dusk

into the night
a pauline twist
much misunderstood

sentences rewritten…
a direction
apostles refused to go

stuffed
with phrases
wasted and postponed

words
like winds
and polluted halls

one moment mute…
then saying things
that were not meant to be said

the prophet's talk…
no longer heard
in hollowed sound

o' what
did the dragon
of darkness breed

madness
cold, impure
divinely undisturbed

who will part that drape
of holy horns
crushed beneath the dust

where
guilt's the ghost
and every word's a mask

maligned
before kings…
and evil's left behind

the forest's shiver
once consecrated…
stands mythless, diabolic and numb

Man creates his earth in terms of his heaven.
As he believes, so does he see, and as he sees, so is his earth.

—Milton Percival, *William Blake's Circle of Destiny*

L I I

the somber maze

one can never
describe the world… nor
protest
against the chaos

existence unfolds
sets a trap
transcends
in customary circles

the circle
more plausible
than
standing still

we see through a glass
darkly
burning unrest…
the instant of the catastrophe

the revolt…
the world
is no longer
guided by saturn

see my shadow
in the sun
built
in the skies of spain

where
the physical
sooner or later
disintegrates

and the movement
of time
is banished
in an inverse form

the phantom
of imagination
down the passage
that we did not wish to take

lifting heavy feet
in clumsy shoes
monstrous prodigy
against this invented world

a mist envelopes
brooding woods
thrusting hands
are tired and torn

through
tangled gloom
roaming through
the somber maze

a wire-thin strip
of existence
where even god's
an accident

*I am an enemy of the New Testament. My enmity is lifelong,
and intensifies as I study its texts more closely.*

—Harold Bloom

LIII

the height of the soul

the only escape
is into words
in a scribbled form
with quilted pen

between
prophet's lines…
subtracted thoughts…
inscribed in lies

we crush
we destroy
we dare to reach
our voyage there

concealed
under cloaks of grey
half-stoic…
unconcerned

writing down
what's inside the world…
fleeing
to concealment

where tragedy
ceases to look
tragic…
it swells in silence

before
the dusk is dark
and you embrace
the hollow ghost

in the wilderness
of years
you have listened
chained and bound

where lines were drawn
without knowing why
and words were said
in another's voice

i have grown old…
bootless
and groping
as the gods grew young

mistaken
for what i'm not
ah… there
is the height of the soul

But when even Bellerophon came to be hated by all the gods, he wandered all desolate and dismayed upon the Aleian plain, devouring his own soul, and shunning the paths of men...

—Homer, *Iliad*

LIV

empty room

impotent rage
and discontent
kindled
by the holy rite

low in reverence
frenzied
by the dream he dreamed
with threats and flames

literalism
crept into
mystery
the prophet withdrawn

strangled tyranny
ignorance
inner sancta
violated and ignored

sanctity grimaced
pale, cold
gray concept nets
a hole in reason

—Alvin Boyd Kuhn

LV

of the christos

the salvific thought
calmly bleeds
drifting down
unto itself

an arc of journeys
that never began
cut out
of a segment of time

staring eyes
go empty
a silent choir
of ignorance

frayed strands
of the primeval truth
the loose
and tangled threads

transformation of
the christos
into a
son of man

as the mountains
are undermined…
exploded
and shattered

tablets
and texts
despoiled motifs
and gilded shrines

the cave
of stillness
ghostly
and hidden

open
the doorways
unravel the riddles
of two-thousand years

study
the dragons
in an ocean
of a billion worlds

sink
beneath the surface
and disappear
like the fable

let the profane
becomes sacred
let myths…
stand outside their words

i saw eternity
the other night
driven
by the spheres

the alter
was naked
the printed word
today exposed

swords and blindfolds
ritual play-acting
toked
and dazzled

along the black walls...
forever sighs
i hear the lonely
wind of god

o' holy fable
theatrical odyssey
i bend my knee...
has thy kingdom come

Those who lack discrimination may quote the letter of the Scripture, but they are really denying its inner truth.

—The BhagavadGita

LVI

of the christos (Part 2)

in
an air of ease
and gentleness
i am issa

i have come

to provide a feeling of help
to the helpless
and the comfort of hope
to the hopeless

from the indus river
to ravalpindi
i ran over the pendjab
the land of the five rivers

i visited the golden temple
of amritsa
the tomb of the king of pendjab
and turned toward kachmyr

the valley
of eternal bliss
descended to
the river djeloum

the waters of which
flow gracefully
between rocky walls
whose tops reach
the azure skies

it has been written
of my miracles
in artificial narrations
constructed from tradition

profoundly
sedimented
into
your imagination

yet my life…
is a painting
my acts shall be captured
as in a sculpture

theologians
have hidden me
the mountains
are being undermined
exploded and shattered

yet, you must go forth
to the hidden chamber
draw my breath in tight…
enter into a mysteriousness
which lies within

so misinterpreted
and misunderstood…
enter the cave of stillness
ghostly in hidden meaning

beyond dreams
between thoughts

dance
as the rain falls upon you face
as the hactin paints the mounds of sand
before you

where distinction between life and death
is dissolved
here… you will meet
the mysterium tremendum of the unknown

where you will hear
a thousand voices reply
and hear the forest tremble
in a world of emptiness

you shall worship the sun
but
if the sun does not exist
you shall worship nature

and if nature does not exist
you shall worship the stars
today you have listened
heard my words
let them become sweet as honey
inside of you

I all alone beweep my outcast state,
And trouble deaf heaven with my bootless cries...

—Shakespeare

prayer

shall i pray
shall i then listen
for the shadow
of a sound

where stillness
is broken up
in the crucifixion
of my cerebral life

shipwrecked
i will go
from wave to wave…
adventure the infinite

i stand
on the border
between the magician
and the priest

in the darkness
of the north
invading the depth
of solemnity

even before me
in the divine fiat
though quiet
and subdued

there inside me
arises a moment
palpable
and intense

interrupting
linear time…
a constellation
of meanings and images

with beating heart
and streaming eyes
i called the phantoms
of a thousand hours

dashed hopes
of high talk…
i was not heard
i saw them not

By the decree of the angels and by the command of holy men, we excommunicate, expel, curse and damn Baruch de Espinoza, with the consent of God... with the 613 precepts which are written therein...

—from the text of excommunication, July 27, 1656

LVIII

spinoza

blackened words
upon a dulling page
wounded hands
that shake and bleed

near the
amstel damns…
of pallid
and gentle cast

unprinted silence
in a double dream
under a broken sky
and staring eyes

o' thy soul…
there you stood
detached
in measurelessness

writings dense
marked and opaque
were scratches and scrolls
of oceans space

like lines
of a hand
written and moved
to reverence…

fragmented
and distracted…
those heresies
and monstrosities

no transcendence
no beliefs
no hopes
no desires

the harlot's cry
from street to street
day after day
in circular time

yet… truth rang through
this unquiet dream
thou messenger
of sympathies

you understood
but did not fall
into the weariness…
of irony

As Judea had given Christianity ethics, and Greece had given it theology, so now Rome gave it organization; all these, with a dozen absorbed and rival faiths, entered into the Christian synthesis. It was not merely that the Church took over some religious customs and forms common in pre-Christian Rome—the stole and other vestments of pagan priests, the use of incense and holy water in purifications, the burning of candles and an everlasting light before the altar, the worship of the saints, the architecture of the basilica, the law of Rome as a basis for canon law, the title of Pontifex Maximus for the Supreme Pontiff, and, in the fourth century, the Latin language as the noble and enduring vehicle of Catholic ritual.

—Will Durant, *Caesar and Christ:*
The Story of Civilization, Volume III

heirs and prodigals

changeability
of existence
behold the stream…
its many windings

behind
pure reflections…
or are we
in its midst

metaphor
of love and torture
actualities
of the imagination

looking down
from its mountain
the conversion
of the i

without the image
without number
always opens
to thy wonder

a characteristic
of essence
to want to
come into being

traps fall before you
foothills echo
through the wide sphere
of vagueness

literary vandals
casts their pearls
with deities….
cast in their own mold

the archetypes…
changing names
that we have seen
a thousand times before

the eternal form
contradictory in essence
altered the writing
as brittle as heirs and prodigals

... the Gospels of the New Testament were really the old dramatic books of the Essenes, from pre-Christian days.

—Eusebius, the bishop of Caesarea

L X

the essene

orphic temples
once woven
into the
construct of thought

mysteries
disintegrated
through the defluxion
of their strength

i caught a glimpse
of what once was
before the saints
distorted and suppressed

disintegrated words
into empty
and deceptive
shape and form

if the storm
were to subside
and the thunder
were to pass

and the uncut rocks
and hidden pages
were mortared…
and opened before us

the symbolism
and irony
the ancient creeds
and the misconceived

the singled out
threads of order
the tapestry…
of thy orphic, thy mosaic

if that breathless void
where silence
as an echo
faded away

before the
darkened skies
o' the silent rain
of ashes

would be
the suffering that eclipsed
the hermetic, the gnostic
and the essene

The truth is that the Gospels are indeed the old manuscripts of the dramatized rituals of the incarnation and resurrection of the sun god Osiris/Horus, rituals that were first Egyptian, later Gnostic and Hellenic, then Hebrew, and finally adopted ignorantly by the Christian movement and transferred to the arena of history.

—Tom Harpur

LXI

warfare of my soul

my soul
treads the
ascending spiral

experiences alternating
between the sunshine
and the shade

my inner spirit
thirsting in the grip
of madness

a bridge
over barren stream
through connecting rooms of time

the invisible
inner world
to the world of outer forms

displaying
a naked bliss
beyond the senses

ripples
on the surface of life
produced by unsuspected springs

a semblance of truth
procuring shadows
of the imagined

the arrow falls
where it will
i can only follow

it strikes me
into triangles
of discontinuity

it thrives
close to the dragon
between the real and the tale

that willing
suspension
of disbelief

obsessions
within the myths…
the core of truth

sweet forms
wrapped
in white robes

ah… let the evening waves
respond
in whispers from the shore

cries of my soul
of osiris
passed to zion's psalms

the inspired prisoner
and warfare
of my soul

Isis and the child Horus were straightway identified with Mary the Virgin and her Son, and in the apocryphal literature of the first few centuries which followed the evengelization of Egypt, several of the legends about Isis and her sorrowful wandering were made to center around the Mother of Christ.

—British Egyptologist, E. A. W. Budge

LXII

o' mother of god

spread the splendor
of the sun
the ever-toiling
of your own sight

i heard
that a woman
ascended
the august skies

in that remote
zodiacal
cluster…
patchwork in the sky

shedding
question'd looks
o' did their spear
pierce thy son

a throne
now empty
that men should weep
and bleed, and groan

darkness shook
the hollow shore
its thousand echoes
casting mythic shrines

the interruption
of the sacred
desacralization
of truth

swooping of fire
across precious stones
battle for
the conflicted

of unawakened thought…
silence
of a tempest's birth…
that faith in portents

time's unquiet flow
in secret chambers
bless me father
as you read, and weep

languished, disintegrated
disappeared
o' has the truth
become unveiled

drink deep
o' mary
a goddess' color
o' mother, isis

and your child
horus
swaddling bands…
myth be thy manger

neith
of sais
theotokos
o' mother of god

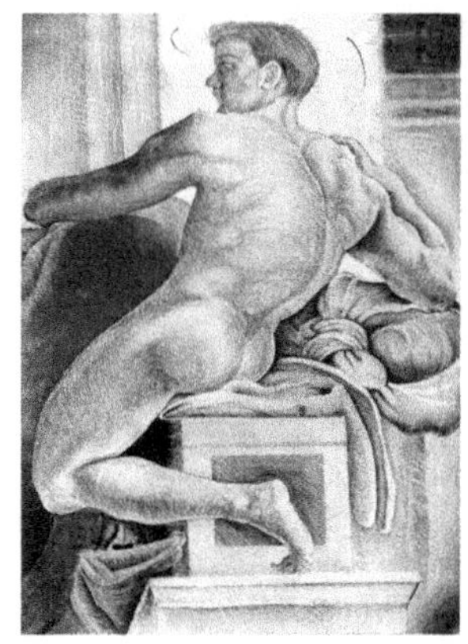

*Nietzsche stresses that the Übermensch is a human being
who overcomes, rises above the loss of God, who courageously
lives with the emptiness that faces him in a godless universe…
beyond the realm of religion and morality.*

—Lou von Salome

LXIII

paralysis of disbelief

the awful shadow...
some hidden power
floats though
things unseen

irrational and
confusing signs
ingenious...
empty and abstruse

addressed to
virgins
saints... and
an army of monks

distorted, suppressed... and
shockingly hidden
arguments they could not
consent to abandon

cluttered up
and jumbled
with numberless
devotions

each stroke
of the critic's blade
reveals the
unapprehendable

fraudulent sermons
some faint flavor
of the piety…
of the despised

calamitous tales
plunged into
the darkest
ravines

the unknown
named
by the more
unknown

dark
and uncut
and the deeps
below the waves

there came a stillness
and there came
a storm
and all the oceans

that loom black
into the sky… where
my hands grope
into nothing

delusion
written with scratches
indentations
and scrolls

i awoke
from insensibility
and looked around
a trembling paralysis of disbelief

as history
and belief
and hypothesis…
crumbled away

It is mere prejudice that I am a human being. Yet I've often dwelt among human beings, from the lowest to the highest. Among the Hindus, I was Buddha, in Greece Dionysus—Alexander and Caesar were reincarnations of me.... However, I now come as Dionysus victorious... I also hung on the cross.

—Nietzsche's words during his
final years of mental decline.

LXIV

cries of wonder

in an abrupt encounter
i entered
the company
of the deathless gods

where
forsaken mankind
was hurled toward me
with unexpected discontinuity

proclaimed openly
and unhesitatingly
desire to deny… to believe
and to doubt well

let not ignorance
get the upper hand
while battling for
the conflicted respite

the determinism
of the physical
the hollowness
of thy thinking

create silence
in order to say
that which is
impossible

o' those wretched men
skilled to plead
with a superficial
set of sophisms

the desacralization
of truth
the swooping
of fire

keep the kaleidoscope
from rotating away
then let the words
return

let them slide
gently
imperceptibly
from what is old

within the interiority
of the chaotic
into the nothingness
of the night

as the land stretches
to the horizon
fully escaping
cries of wonder

where true being
does not lie hidden…
but rages
far above you

far from
the wide-pathed earth
across the
precious stones

i entered
the forest where
the goddess diana
was cast

the huntress
misinterpreted
the anchor
rudely torn

amidst
insuperable riddles…
o' who will take
this candle from my hand

That which is known as the Christian religion existed among the ancients, and never did not exist; from the very beginning of the human race until the time when Christ came in the flesh, at which time the true religion, which already existed, began to be called Christianity.

—St. Augustine

LXV

canonized in majesty

witoba
krishna, horus

man of flesh
accreted
of drama and myth

man
of seven bodies
with hidden forces

within the frame
of the hellenic…
the esoteric

o' the cult
of bethlehem
and calvary

propounded
by greek…
by uproar and tumult

swooping
over fire
and precious stones

figure
undefiled…
of the ever-coming

of the solar cult
from age
to age

the backward movement
long hand
of the eternal

arise and pass
always becoming…
but never being

consigned to silence
the transcendental
without end

pull aside
the veil
of the imagined

shrouded in him
the puzzling
and perplexed

given shape
voice and name
to spectral terror

the altars fall
as the pious stand…
heads bowed low

shafts
of falsehood…
cease to be

has not the whirlwind
of our spirit driven
truth's deathless germs

to thought's to
remotest caves
among the stars

the sons of earth
to foul idols
once knelt and prayed

and gray priests
o' they triumphed…
formal, fixed and decreed

canonized
in majesty…
o' thy spiritual tale

It will stand in the present work as the firing of the opening gun in a battle that will be waged from now on to unseat from its throne of power in the domain of mass consciousness that weird and fantastic delusion of literalized and historicized Scriptural myths which has steeped the minds of untold millions in doltish superstition over so many centuries...

—Alvin Boyd Kuhn

LXVI

misshapened shadows

various worlds
winds that creep
human hearts
and a vacant face

peaks joined as one…
the cliffs stood
as unmoved
as before

the play of forces
as i had known
dictating
the terms of fate

archetypes
of the soul
a wasteland of
meaningless

fear and dream
of demons, ghosts
and o'
the death before you go

if it could not be…
if it had not been
and thy spells
did not bind

a process…
contained within
a body of myths
in the triad of night

echoing vaults
a faith
nursed by fear
of misshapened shadows

*Sometimes, however, the footprints are so hidden that
the power of human intelligence cannot reach them.*

—Giles of Viterbo

LXVII

the frozen glaze

dark things
between the shadow
and the soul

to the last syllable
of recorded time

who live
in furnished souls

cornerless…
in my room
i rest

and for small reason
think the world
as imagined

out of the indifferences
with which we forget
each other
and at times, ourselves

and ask
are god
and my imagination… one

far away
beyond an interrupted cry
the grains
beyond age

in shreds of mist
and thy humbling dark

o' harp and altar
of the fury fused

free sweep of spirit...
its own bridge
to intelligence

dissent
looming thick
allegory of the logos-monad

a singular aberration
springing up
from the conditions of the times

misconception
of the high truth
absurd and impossible

alleged veridical events
unconscionable contortions...
of ideas given to man

predications of allegory
wrenched away

in the perfervid regions
of deluded belief

o' what has it meant
to two millennia
of darkness

this misjudgment
of fishermen

a darkness
profound and universal

eerie glow of the stirring
among the buried embers
of an extinguished blaze

for the moments
of despair
over the fact that nothing
is becoming

drop the reins
before the infinite

wrestle
for sun and light
unriddle the soul

let prayer and curse
become the ghost
that wanders over the frozen glaze

Unfortunately, instances of possibly inaccurate translation, bias comments assumptions and speculations and this innocently blend into explanations of attitude and beliefs of ancient times. Male bias, together with preconceived religious attitudes, which appears in both major and minor matters, raises some very pressing and pertinent questions concerning the objectivity of the analysis of the archaeological and historical material available at present. It suggests that long accepted theories and conclusions must be reexamined, reevaluated and where indicated by actual evidence, revised.

—Merlin Stone, *When God Was a Woman*

LXVIII

she

listen
hear the grating roar
as waves draw back
begin and cease

then begin again

find also
in the sound of thought
hearing it
by the distant sea

the sea of faith

once, at the full…
today
i only hear its long
withdrawing roar

its clash and fight

confused alarms
of struggle
and flight…
o' ignorant one

wisdom misapplied

a misty dream
emerges
for a while
night is at hand

my darkened mind lays hold

i awoke
and the dawn was grey
i cried for madder music
i begged for stronger wine

before a brew of untruth

stiff and sore
and scarred
i took away
my hand

the myths have failed

enlightenment
abandoned
interpretations
filtered through minds unschooled

expression twisted

mental
aberration
engendered by
misconception

now....

listen
hear the grating roar
as waves draw back
begin and cease

then begin again

worship
without lifting eyes
above the earth…
the grass and trees

she is resident
in every oak, pine
flower, spring and vale
the sunshine and the rain

The education itself, by which, according to these generally judicious writers, the youthful mind was to be impregnated with reverential feelings for the objects of national worship, must have been coldly conducted by teachers conscious that they were practicing a pious fraud upon their disciples, and perpetually embarrassed by the necessity of maintaining gravity befitting such solemn subjects, and of suppressing the involuntary smile which might betray the secret of their own impiety.

—Dean Milman

LXVIX

the last god

summer winds
once crept…
visits
with an inconstant glance

records of the vain
doubt, chance
and mutability…
sudden shadows fallen

wondering
between two worlds
reason at defiance
flourished in elaborate rites

high-pitched consecrations
deflated…
the stones
lie unmoved

yet a new universe
rushes in
i am measuring candlelight
by other candles…

o' there is magic
as though in battles
a subterranean upheaval
through simple rhythms

transformed
by counter effects…
my being, itself
as nothing

measurements of its space
the events of its past
like the lines of a hand
written on the corners of the streets

becoming
a passageway
a reflection
of strange forms

entering
into the dangerous region
transcending
into the unhiddenness

kneeling
to another
of our kind
that lived two-thousand years ago

in the main
of egyptian lore
stripped of celestial glories…
of poverty on earth

to the inner richness
of the grounds and abysses
in the site of the moment
the lightening up and concealment

from the heights of heaven
to its wintry immersion
in the round of death
and limitation in darkness

the flame to seize
the veil to rend
a soul upthrown
to hide the orb and every throne

from the marking out
the sacred space
and a home
for the gods

to the penning
of madmen's ravings
then twisted
into mésalliance

o' companions in delusion
bound together
ruthless inquisitors
ignorance, warped and deformed

history
as a storage room
for costumes…
arbitrary narrowness and secrecy

behold the gateway
two paths
forward and back
i look… and see no end

intervening shadows
damp depressions
curtains of darkness
and drifting clouds

is the last god
the end
or…
the other beginning

Religions try to protect one from losing oneself. By contrast, mystical experiences feed on 'loss' and it is this that they transform into gain. In the throes of mystical experience, one finds oneself in a state of such unexpected and unprecedented coherence as if encountering one's identity for the first time. Meanwhile, one also feels forsaken: the transcendence of the self-interrogates the very sense of identity. For this reason, such experiences are paradoxical: one achieves ipseity at the very point when this union is the least fathomable. Such experiences reveal the contradictory nature of human life: one is the least in charge over the single thing that is the utmost proof of existence—one's own life.

—László F. Földényi, *The Glance of the Medusa*

LXX

matrix of the myth

pilate saith
what is truth
throwing off language
in its wateriness

trampling
the grapes obscure
of the disparate…
that which has been withdrawn

unmasking falsehood
a detachment
working backward
on the verge of its presence

advancing
with measured steps
where the locomotives of sleep
rust

whispers in darkness
are noiselessly squashed
as something
long since known

a nightmare
of undigested ideologies
cherished in the cult
of mysteries

stand before me
where there are no sounds
and rhythms
do not dance

o' liberator
wrapped in shackles
words tied to a tree…
and your rented sky

i pulled apart
the blocks of your tale
rearranged the spaces
of your shadowplay

dogmatic aberrations
a series of decentrings
an imaginary
reflection

annihilating totality
deported borders
and fragments
reserved for nothingness

shattering
the logic of beginnings
dominated by confusion…
the matrix of the myth

... far more removed from the power of man's comprehension, was the state of non-being, when the Deity beyond being, without thinking, or feeling, or determining, or choosing, or being compelled, or desiring, willed to create universality.

—Basilides

LXXI

the gulf of hell

garrulous sorcerer
mourning the beyond
the grove
where our fathers' spirits passed

a barren altar
and trail overgrassed
a mirror
dimmed by tears

the outer world
dwindles
and day fades
from day

a thousand knees
are bent
ten thousand years
naked, fasting… praying

upon this barren mountain
where storm is perpetual…
and cannot move
the gods they've made

scribbled insanity
and nonsense
trumpeted…
immortal wisdom

where outer events
are shadows
in my
inner world

unintelligible gibberish
abstruse allegory
the passion
extended backwards

this persuasion
of acceptance
to warped
and eager minds

at that throne
the traitors summoned
like roaring
kings in truth

took their royal seat
their soul's revenge
did not dare
look back

heard one stifled prayer
before the god they made…
there is famine
in this gulf of hell

and i believed
the myth
dear good moon
forgive me

Like a waterfall of thousands of roaring torrents which plunged down from the sky, eternally, eternally poured forth without a momentary pause, without a second's peace, thus it sounded in his ears and all his senses were intently focused solely on this. His labouring anguish became more and more caught up and carried away in the whirlpool of this wild confusion.

—Wilhelm Heinrich Wackenroder

LXXII

sea of doubt

i glare
in the distance
where the friar's face
is shadowed and dark

i hear the echoes
that vanish behind…
the dizziness
that threatens the mind

in the naked night
myriads came
to quench
the flame

world of moods
voices trembled
and circled
the fictitious vanishing point

passages torn
context lost
letters altered
words cut in half

patchwork
of fragments
twisted, distorted
in the sewers of myth

mystery dramas
devoid of sanctity
erected upon delusions…
scribbled insanity… raging pages turn

forgotten temples
images led in…
overcome
and left unknown

an angel
crushed under foot…
the church
at its side

tongues lose possession
throwing off language
in its wateriness
everything original is flattened down

outer veil drifting
a thousand worlds beyond
the footprints are hidden
in a sea of doubt

all truth
is crooked
time itself
is a circle

these paths
they offend…
raphael
without hands

where the evil dragon
hydra
lies in wait
to devour the babe

Auden, W. H.. *Lectures on Shakespeare*, Princeton University Press, 2019

Badiou, Alain, *Infinite Thought*, Continuum, 2003

Bloom, Harold. *The Bright Book of Life*, Knopf Doubleday Publishing Group, 2020

Corngold, Stanley. *Walter Kafmann*, Princeton University Press, 2019

Das Nibelungenlied: Song of the Nibelungs, Yale University Press, 2006

Durant, Will. *Caesar and Christ: The Story of Civilization, Volume III*, Simon & Schuster, 1950

Durant, Will. *The Age of Faith: The Story of Civilization, Volume IV*, Simon & Schuster, 1950

Ehrman D., Bart, *Lost Christianities*, Oxford University Press, 2003

Földényi, László F.L. *Melancholy (The Margellos World Republic of Letters)*, Yale University Press, 2016

Földényi, László F.. *The Glance of the Medusa (The Hungarian List)* Seagull Books, 2020

George, Stefan, *The Works of Stefan George*, University of North Carolina Press, 1974

Guignebert, Charles. *The Jewish World in the Time of Jesus*, Barakaldo Books, 2022

Harpur, Tom. *The Pagan Christ: Is blind faith killing Christianity?* Allen and Unwin, 2004

Hillman, James, *RE-Visioning Psychology*, Harper and Row, 1976

Kaufmann, Walter, *Critique of Religion and Philosophy*, Princeton University Press, 1979

Kaufmann, Walter, *Goethe, Kant and Hegel*, McGraw Hill Book Company, 1980

Kaufmann, Walter, *The Faith of a Heretic*, Princeton University Press, 2015

Kuhn, Alvin Boyd. *Shadow of the Third Century: A Revaluation of Christianity*, Papamoa Press, 1949

Mallarme, Stephane, *Divagations*, University of Chicago Press, 1981

Maritain, Berdyaev, Buber and Tillich, *Four Existential Theologians*, Greenwood Press, 1975

Massey, Gerald. *Ancient Egypt, The Light of the World*, Martino Publishing, 1907

Milosz, O.V. de L., *The Noble Traveller*, Lindisfarne Press, 1985

Nietzsche, Friedrich, *Unfashionable Observations*, Stanford University Press, 1995

Nietzsche, Friedrich, *Thus Spoke Zarathustra*, Modern Library Edition, 1995

Pagels, Elaine. *The Gnostic Gospels*, Random House Publishing Group, 1979

Percival, Milton O., *William Blake's Circle of Destiny*, Columbia University Press, 1938

Raine, Kathleen, *Blake and the New Age*, Routledge, 2013

Rosen, Stanley, *The Mask of Enlightenment, Nietzsche's Zarathustra*, Cambridge University Press, 1995

Rowland, Ingrid D. *Giordano Bruno*, Farrar, Straus and Giroux, 2008

Salome, Lou, *Nietzsche*, University of Illinois Press, 2001

Sartre, Jean-Paul, *Being and Nothingness*, Washington Square Press, 1943

Schopenhauer, Arthur, *The World as Will and Representation* – Volume 1, Dover Publications, 1966

Solomon, Robert C., *From Hegel to Existentialism*, Oxford University Press, 1987

Vesey, Godfrey, *Understanding Wittgenstein*, Cornell University Press, 1974

Vickers, Julia. *Lou von Salome*, McFarland & Company, Inc., Publishers, 2008

Watson, Peter, *The Age of Atheists*, Simon and Schuster, 2014

Zaretsky, Robert, *A Life Worth Living: Albert Camus and the Quest for Meaning*, Belknap Press, 2016

Zweig, Stefan, *Three Masters, Balzac, Dicken and Dostoeffsky*, Forgotten Books, 2012

Zweig, Stefan, Struggle with the Daemon, Pushkin Press, 2012

9 7 9 8 8 8 6 7 9 3 2 2 2